New Zealand
in Colour

By the same authors:

Michael King:

Moko: Maori Tattooing in the Twentieth Century
Make It News: How to Approach the Media
Te Ao Hurihuri (ed.)
Tihe Mauri Ora (ed.)
Te Puea
New Zealand: Its Land and its People
New Zealanders at War
The Collector: A Biography of Andreas Reischek

Martin Barriball:

New Zealand: Images, Impressions
The Mobil Illustrated Guide to New Zealand (with Jeremy and Diana Pope)
The North Island in Colour (with Mervyn Dykes)
The South Island in Colour (with Mervyn Dykes)

New Zealand
in Colour

Text Michael King

Photographs Martin Barriball

REED METHUEN

First published 1982
Reprinted 1983, 1985, 1986, 1987

REED METHUEN PUBLISHERS LTD
39 Rawene Road, Auckland 10

ISBN 0 474 00239 X

Typeset by Jacobsen Typesetters Ltd
Printed by Everbest Printing Co Ltd, Hong Kong

Contents

Introduction

To the Europeans who rediscovered and settled it, New Zealand was a beautiful but alien land. The recurring note was struck by Abel Tasman. In 1642 the Dutchman became the first known non-Polynesian navigator to sight the country. His sailors clashed with Maoris at Golden Bay after a misunderstanding about trumpet playing (Tasman believed a Maori challenge to fight was simply a display of musical prowess, and he answered it); four seamen were killed. Tasman then sailed the length of the North Island's west coast without landing, seeing only sand dunes and the likelihood of further hostile receptions. He left New Zealand convinced that the country was an inhospitable desert peopled by violent savages.

James Cook did something to redress the balance in the eighteenth century. He found lush harbours and befriended the inhabitants, and his charting of the coast and detailed journal observations led to British colonisation in the nineteenth century. But it still took a long time for European migrants to feel at home in the Antipodes. Most came from the British Isles — from England, Scotland and Ireland. Unlike the handful of continental Europeans, the British were neither drawn nor exalted by mountainous parts of the country. They sought landscapes that seemed most like Britain. And they enhanced the similarity by planting exotic trees and flowers, by introducing English birds, and by constructing English-looking churches and cottages. They tried to transplant what was familiar to them as a means of insulating themselves from what was unfamiliar and therefore frightening.

Right up to the 1950s New Zealand school children learnt a poem that began, "Land of the moa and Maori, land of the kowhai and kauri" — as if these features were strange in the country of their origin. And a nationally recognised poet spoke of "what great gloom stands in a land of settlers with never a soul at home".

The result was that New Zealand became far more than a land of extraordinarily varied landscape. Within that landscape vegetation, fauna and mixed architectural styles created still further diversity. Untamed South Island lakes, backdropped by mountains and virgin forest, contrast with manicured city ones featuring stately willows and white swans. Sections of highway bounded by rimu, kahikatea and kowhai are succeeded by others lined with rhododendrons and camelias. Pastureland is as likely to be dotted with poplars and macrocarpa as it is with cabbage tree and ponga. Rivers surge mightily from rock gorges and meander elsewhere through daffodil-lined banks. And throughout the country native fantails, tui and silvereyes compete in gardens with blackbirds, thrushes and sparrows. Flora, fauna and landscape are every bit as thoroughly colonised and variegated as the country's inhabitants.

The native Maori population has been the constant witness to these changes. Arriving in New Zealand more than 1,200 years ago, Maoris were always more intimately at home there than later migrants. They necessarily lived closer to the land and its seasons because they brought so little with them in canoe voyages. They depended on wild roots, on birds, on fish and shellfish, on some cultivated crops, and on the wood and stone that were the basis for their material culture and the media for their increasingly complex artistic expression.

Being neolithic and illiterate they carried with them only language, traditions, a few vegetables, some stone and wooden tools, a species of dog and the Polynesian rat. Everything else and everything subsequent that was life-sustaining they had to take from the New Zealand soil. Even their traditions became New Zealand-centred as they made the rapid transition from migrants to tangata whenua, people of the land.

When Europeans appeared the Maori experimented with successive modes of rejection, welcome, further rejection, and finally a reluctant and then a confident compromise with the culture and technology of the new colonists. Their numbers plummeted close to extinction in the late nineteenth century and then rose sharply in the twentieth as they acquired immunity from European diseases and strengthened Maori cultural roots by a controlled accommodation of Western culture. They remain a constant reminder that New Zealand is a Pacific rather than a European nation — in the meeting houses and pa scattered over the North Island, in the literal colour of the Polynesian faces, and in the proverbial colour which Maori values and customs bring to the nation's more staid Anglo-Saxon habits. As a component of the national life the Maori element now waxes rather than wanes.

Up to and immediately after World War II Europeans in New Zealand still referred to England as "home". It took them a long time to feel that they and the fauna they brought with them belonged in the new country. Since the 1940s their numbers have been swollen further by immigrants from countries such as Greece, Poland, Holland, India, China and Cambodia, and from the Pacific Islands.

By the 1980s, Pakeha — the Maori word for stranger — had ceased to mean "outsider". It now refers simply to non-Polynesian New Zealanders. The components of population remain as diverse as the landscape. But they have ceased to look abroad for identity and inspiration; they now find these things confidently within the borders of their own country. And the literature which used to express disquiet and remoteness from cultural origins now celebrates a nation at home with itself and its own people, Maori and Pakeha.

CAPE REINGA LIGHTHOUSE

The Far North

The Far North

The Far North is in every sense the cradle of European culture in New Zealand — and possibly of Maori culture, too, although this is more difficult to establish. Certainly Maoris were settled in Northland 1,100 years ago, and the earliest traces of agriculture in the country have been found there, in the Bay of Islands. Some scholars are convinced it was the first part of New Zealand to be colonised by Polynesians. They suggest that the canoe migration myths, which most Maori tribes retain, refer not to an ocean journey to New Zealand but to major movements of population out of Northland to southern parts of the country. Today the Ngapuhi, Te Aupouri, Te Rarawa, Te Mahurehure and Ngati Whatua tribes make up a sizable and energetic section of the region's population. They are concentrated mainly in the northern counties, and the most visible signs of their presence are the

marae and meeting houses (many not carved) dotted across the landscape.

Europeans were drawn to Northland in the late eighteenth century. Traders, whalers and adventurers homed in on the Bay of Islands as a major South Pacific port. It gained a reputation for lawlessness and violence. On the west coast Hokianga Harbour also attracted ships seeking shelter, spars and provisions. Incidents such as the burning of the ship *Boyd* by Maoris in Whangaroa Harbour in 1809 brought a degree of notoriety to New Zealand.

In 1814 an Anglican missionary, Samuel Marsden of Sydney, preached to Maoris for the first time and later established a mission at the Bay of Islands. Other denominations — especially Wesleyans and Roman Catholics — followed and also began their evangelising in the Far North. With them they brought agriculture and literacy, believing that their task was to civilise the Maoris in addition to saving their souls.

The Bay of Islands also became the country's first administrative centre. A British Resident, James Busby, was appointed in 1833 to see to the interests of British subjects, and it was largely as a consequence of his reports that the colony's first Lieutenant-Governor, Captain William Hobson, arrived there in 1840 to effect a treaty with the Maoris. The Treaty of Waitangi was carried throughout the country, but was initially signed in front of Busby's residence in the Bay of Islands. It offered the natives the protection of the British Crown in return for their ceding the sovereignty of the country to Queen Victoria. It led to the annexation of New Zealand by Britain the same year, and to the establishment of the colony's first capital near Kororareka, the present township of Russell.

From the 1840s the economic and administrative importance of Northland declined. The capital was transferred to Auckland. There was a boom in kauri timber and kauri gum, but both were ruthlessly exploited and depleted. Northland diminished in national importance and its quiet communities — with the exception of Whangarei — now attract tourists rather than investment capital.

1. Cape Reinga was known to the Maori as Te Rerenga Wairua — the place where the spirits of the dead leap into the Underworld. Beyond it lies Cape Maria van Diemen, named in 1642 by the Dutch navigator Abel Tasman after the wife of his sponsor.

2. Buses drive up Northland's Ninety Mile Beach and stop to allow passengers to stroll on its open sands.

3. To the east, Whangaroa Harbour's hills provide both an ideal anchorage for small craft and shelter for holiday cottages.

3

1

2

1. Russell, known formerly as Kororareka, is close to the site of the country's first capital. It was a favourite port for whalers and adventurers from the late 1700s. According to one writer, the orgies there were "such as would defile the pages of history". New Zealand's first Vice-Regal representative, Captain William Hobson, set up his capital at nearby Okiato in 1840, and a Union Jack was flown from the hill above Russell township. In 1844 a war in the north was precipitated when a Ngapuhi chief dissatisfied with British rule chopped down the flagstaff. Fighting followed between Maori and British Imperial troops. In 1845 the flagstaff was cut down twice more, and in March of that year Russell was sacked and burnt with a loss of 13 European lives. The dissident Maoris were finally defeated at Ruapekapeka in January 1846. The residents of Russell returned and rebuilt their township. Now it is the administrative and holiday centre for the Bay of Islands. In particular it acts as a base for the district's popular big-game fishing, which includes marlin and shark admired throughout the world for their magnitude. Russell is also the point of departure for sight-seeing and other fishing trips around the harbour. It is linked by launch services to Paihia and Opua across the bay.

2. Piercy Island off Cape Brett in the Bay of Islands has a famous hole in the rock through which boats can sail. In naming it after Admiralty official Sir Piercy Brett, Captain James Cook was also enjoying a pun.

1

2

3

1. A unique feature of the Bay of Islands is Kelly Tarlton's Shipwreck Museum on board the barque ***Tui*** at Paihia. Underwater archaeology did not exist in New Zealand until Tarlton and his friend Wade Doak began to look for and explore New Zealand wrecks in the 1960s.

2. Exhibits include pieces of ships, maritime equipment, jewellery (including relics of the Rothschild Collection) and some of the first wrist watches.

3. A special feature of the collection is gold jewellery and coins salvaged from the ***Elingamite*** and ***Tasmania*** wrecks. The ***Elingamite***, object of Tarlton's first major expedition, ran on to rocks and sank off the Three Kings Islands in November 1902. Forty-five people drowned in the disaster. Tarlton and Doak recovered a large number of coins from the ship's submerged skeleton. The ***Tasmania*** went down off Mahia Peninsula in 1897 with a loss of 13 lives. In the case of both wrecks, a large part of their interest lay in the discovery of passengers' personal effects.

4. Kerikeri Inlet on the northern side of the Bay of Islands is a fine anchorage. It is the site of the second Anglican mission station in the country, established there in 1819. Opposite the mission settlement stood Kororipo, home pa of the notorious Ngapuhi fighting chief Hongi Hika. Hongi visited England and Australia in 1820 and 1821 and returned to Kerikeri with over 1,000 muskets. He armed his warriors with them and went south to subjugate the tribes of the North Island. He was largely successful because his adversaries had not acquired muskets.

5. Kerikeri today is the centre of New Zealand's largest citrus-growing area. The old stone store, built in 1833, is now a museum. Next to it is the country's oldest building, the Kemp homestead, built for the mission in 1819. The following year the Anglicans there introduced the plough to New Zealand.

4

5

1

2

1-3. Maori costume is most likely to be seen nowadays on ceremonial occasions: headbands, sashes and piupiu (flax skirts) for the men; these and bodices for the women. Most of the woven material is decorated with colourful taniko patterns. On such occasions — and this one commemorates the signing of the Treaty of Waitangi in February 1840 — Maoris provide challenges, haka (posture dances) and action songs. The men are loud, aggressive performers; the women specialise in soft lilting music, often accompanied by hand and arm movements or by actions with the traditional poi. Without contributions of this kind New Zealand would be largely devoid of colourful ceremony. At Waitangi Day celebrations Maoris are joined by sailors of the Royal New Zealand Navy, who complement Polynesian grace with their own more disciplined formations.

3

4. The Maori meeting house at Waitangi is unusual in that its carvings represent the ancestors and designs of all Maori tribes, not simply those of the local Ngapuhi. These panels were carved in the 1930s by a team from all over the country. The meeting house itself was intended as a national marae or forum, emphasising the respect with which Maoris hold Waitangi as the place where their ancestors solemnly ceded the sovereignty of the country to the British Crown. While some have questioned the validity of the treaty in subsequent years, the majority still regard it as the symbol and cornerstone of Maori–Pakeha co-operation.

5. Another Maori site close to Waitangi is Rewa's model village near Kerikeri, named after Hongi Hika's second-in-command. This complex is a re-creation of a pre-European pa with fortifications, palisades, huts, a storehouse and a chief's dwelling. All are made from traditional materials and to traditional designs.

6. The site where the Treaty of Waitangi was first signed is now part of a national memorial. The ceremony took place in front of James Busby's house, known today simply as the Treaty House. Built in the early 1830s it is a fine example of early colonial architecture. Busby is less well known as New Zealand's first grape grower and wine maker — a tradition that was not to flourish in New Zealand until well into the twentieth century. The house itself was bought by a much-loved Governor-General of New Zealand, Lord Bledisloe, and he donated it to the nation in 1932. It is now the scene of the annual Waitangi Day celebrations and draws thousands of visitors at other times of the year.

4

5

6

1

2

1. Tairua Bay is typical of dozens of sheltered beaches on Northland's east coast. The white sand and quiet blue water fringed by pohutukawa trees and toetoe are characteristic of the area and have made it immensely popular with holiday makers, campers and real-estate agents. All this is in contrast to Northland's west coast. That too has a beauty of its own, but of a far more rugged variety. The open beaches have high dunes, and surf pounds in dangerously. The harbours tend to be muddy and edged with mangroves. The result is that the demand for property and facilities has been higher on the east coast, and the west is less developed and less populous.

2. Inland Northland also holds surprises. The Whangarei Falls close to Whangarei city are set in seven hectares of bush and drop 24 metres into a wide and tree-lined basin. They are one of several tourist targets in the area. Others include the high bluffs of Bream Head at the entrance to Whangarei Harbour, and Kamo Springs to the north of the city.

3. Northland's sub-tropical climate supports many plants that are less likely to grow in other parts of the country. One is the hibiscus, which grows prolifically in gardens throughout the district. Some people have even succeeded in cultivating bananas and pineapples, though not in commercial quantities. Millions of years ago the Far North also supported a New Zealand coconut palm. Although it has long since disappeared as a result of climatic changes, fossilised coconuts with three holes at the base occasionally wash up on Northland beaches.

4. In Northland, as elsewhere throughout the country, wading birds flourish in rivers, swamps and estuaries. One of the most versatile and most graceful is the pied stilt, which enjoys all three environments and is often seen on inland waterways. This one is immature. When it is fully grown its plumage will settle into more sharply contrasting black and white.

3

Auckland

Auckland

Auckland — known as the Queen City — prides itself on being the country's most elegant metropolis, and its most hedonistic one. Its establishment dates from Lieutenant-Governor Hobson's decision to take the capital there in 1841. It retained this status until 1865, a major factor in its early growth. In Hobson's vision it was an ideal site. It lay on an isthmus between two large and sheltered harbours, and because most of the country's trading activities then centred on the northern part of the country, it was close to areas of economic importance. In addition Maori settlement on the isthmus — although it had once been extensive — was thin by 1841. And so Hobson bought the site of the town from the Ngati Whatua owners.

The wisdom of the decision was confirmed by subsequent events, even though the capital eventually went to Wellington. After a brief gold and

agricultural boom in the South Island later in the century, Auckland regained and held the commercial initiative for much of the twentieth century. It has remained the country's largest and most prosperous city. Its industries thrive, its ports continue to ship out agricultural produce and manufactured goods, and to import those items which the country is unable to make itself. Equally important, Auckland's climate and room for unlimited growth have pulled in residents and businesses in large numbers.

The range of lifestyle options which the city offers are important to Aucklanders and to visitors alike. There are two harbours on the city doorstep and four more within a couple of hours' drive. The Hauraki Gulf, protected by the Coromandel Peninsula, offers the safest large area of water in the country for boating and fishing. There are dozens of beaches and bush reserves within easy distance. Auckland is also better endowed with parks — especially the Domain and Cornwall Park — than any other New Zealand community. In summer Aucklanders turn out *en masse* for outdoor recreation — walking, swimming, yachting, fishing. The city is the most outdoor-oriented in the country. It is not surprising, perhaps, that the phenomenon of jogging has caught on here so strongly. The sport's popularity has increased to such an extent that the annual Round the Bays run attracts a crowd of over 80,000, from primary-school children to octogenarians.

Aucklanders are proud of their city, its facilities and its achievements. Its suburbs are the most extensive in the country, and many of them are also the most picturesque, especially those overlooking the sea. The inner city, especially Ponsonby and Herne Bay, is undergoing a renewal and becoming a focal point of the city's nightlife. All this makes them confident, even — sometimes — boastful. But they have much to boast about.

1. Like a great coathanger the harbour bridge links Auckland's North Shore and city. People who once lived hours away from Queen Street can now commute to the heart of town in 10 minutes. High-rise offices in the background are the imprimatur of success shared by prosperous cities the world over.

2. Pohutukawa are among Auckland's most treasured assets. The waterfront drive — here at Kohimarama, and elsewhere — is lined with them. Flowering in December they fully live up to their reputation as the country's own Christmas trees.

3. Mission Bay at summer's height is crammed with sunbathers of all ages. Aucklanders are above all else a beach people.

3

22
30

2

3

4

5

1. Auckland may no longer be the nation's political capital, but it is certainly the yachting capital. More money is spent on boats here than in the rest of the country put together; here too competitions are more numerous and more intense. It is a long-established tradition that brings out yachts in their thousands on the annual Anniversary Day Regatta in January.

2. The Mission Bay fountain flares spectacularly in the dark, one of the gems of Auckland's nightlife.

3. Jogging, which has developed into a national sport, began in Auckland. This happened largely because of the world-famous exploits of local athletes such as Arthur Lydiard, Murray Halberg and Peter Snell. Now joggers are to be seen everywhere in the city at all times of the year — here in Mission Bay or on other beaches, in the city's many parks, or simply along pavements.

4. The sheltered nature of the Hauraki Gulf, its dozens of islands and hundreds of safe beaches, ensures that a considerable proportion of Auckland's resources is tied up in large yachts and launches. This marina at Half Moon Bay on the Tamaki Inlet is only one of many jammed with expensive craft.

5. Waiheke Island is the third largest in the country, discounting the mainland. It is surrounded by idyllic beaches with exotic names such as Palm Beach (shown here, on the island's eastern side), Blackpool, Cowes, Surfdale and Ostend. In addition to holiday makers the island has a large permanent population.

1

2

1. Rangitoto Island, Auckland Harbour and sunrise from Okahu Bay, Orakei. Although the city is built on a chain of volcanoes, Rangitoto is the only one to have erupted within the period of human occupation. Maoris gave it the name, which means "bleeding skies", as a result of witnessing its convulsions. Several Maori villages were buried under its ash, including one on adjacent Motutapu Island. Okahu Bay, now an anchorage for large yachts, was for a long time the refuge of the remnants of the Ngati Whatua tribe, from whom Lieutenant-Governor William Hobson bought the site of Auckland city. The tribe clung to a steadily shrinking pa here until the early 1950s, when members were persuaded to move on to the hill overlooking the bay. On the flat, however, they left their burial ground and a small chapel, the last relics of the old settlement.

2. St Stephen's Church at Judges Bay in Parnell is one of the city's oldest links with its past. Built in 1857, it broods over a fragment of the harbour foreshore which has been kept as it was a century ago. Beyond the grass, the graves and the beach, however, the main trunk railway line, Tamaki Drive and the port's container terminal remind the browser that Auckland has moved far and fast in the limited period of Pakeha settlement.

Provincial North Island

Provincial North Island

Provincial North Island is in every sense the backbone of New Zealand. Its landscape contains every feature that characterises the country as a whole, barring the Southern Alps: snow-capped peaks, bush-clad ranges, a desert plateau, a volcanic crust and thermal activity, sprawling lakes, meandering rivers, rolling hill country, flat pastureland and every possible variety of coastline. The scenery may not be as arresting as that in the alpine south, but it is typical of most of New Zealand.

The same could be said of the people. The population of large centres such as Hamilton, New Plymouth, Wanganui and Gisborne are — literally and metaphorically — middle New Zealand. They preach and practise the virtues of provincial life: hard work, respect for and reliance on primary industry, a strong emphasis on private enterprise and individual rights, a commitment to rugby and

horse racing, and a conservative political orientation. In the smaller rural towns such as Taumarunui, Hawera and Pahiatua, these qualities are even more pronounced. In particular the city visitor is likely to be reminded forcefully that 80 per cent of New Zealand's export income still derives from agriculture. And the dairy farms, sheep runs and cattle stations of the rural North Island are responsible for generating most of it.

Some parts of the island have also come to rely increasingly on tourism for income. The New Zealander's 40-hour week and tradition of paid holidays allows considerable movement within the country, and the age of the jumbo jet is bringing tourists from abroad at the rate of over 300,000 a year (mainly from the United States, Australia, Canada and Japan).

The major area that beckons holiday seekers is the central North Island: Rotorua with its thermal novelties and strongly visible manifestations of Maori culture, and Taupo with trout fishing in its lake and rivers, especially the Tongariro. Other areas, too, have much to offer. The Waitomo Caves provide the most spectacular accessible examples of stalagmites and stalactites in the country. The skiing on Mt Ruapehu's Whakapapa and Turoa fields is admirable. Other mountains and ranges, especially Egmont, provide challenging climbs. The Urewera National Park boasts the largest area of virgin bush in the island and endless opportunities for camping, tramping, fishing and deer stalking. Beach resorts swell in popularity, particularly the sun-drenched shores of the Bay of Plenty and the extraordinary variety of the Coromandel Peninsula.

Provincial North Island also houses the majority of the country's rural Maori population. Although most Maoris now live in cities alongside the Pakeha, it is in country communities that Maori values and institutions — especially those of the marae — are strongest: places such as Ngaruawahia, Ruatoria and Tokaanu, to name a few. These keep the traditional bases for the culture strong and vital.

1. The beach at Whangaroa on the East Cape has a characteristically rugged shore which thrusts into the sea at the country's furthest point east.

2. At the Ruakura Research Centre in Hamilton animals and pasture are under constant study. Funded by the Government, scientists here look for new ways of increasing the efficiency and the output of primary production in New Zealand.

3. Mt Tarawera, brooding over the lake of the same name, was the last New Zealand volcano to erupt on a major scale, in 1886. Today it dominates a landscape that it once devastated with lava and ash.

3

1

2

3

1. The township of Coromandel was a "boom and bust" community. Like the peninsula on which it stands, it was named after the British warship *Coromandel* which called into its harbour for kauri spars in 1820. That visit set the pattern for future development. The settlement swelled in the 1850s as a port from which much Coromandel timber, especially kauri, was shipped out to Auckland and Australia.

In 1852 a sawmiller named Charles Ring discovered gold-bearing quartz close to the township. He rushed at once to Auckland to claim the Provincial Government's £250 prize for the finder of the first "payable" goldfield. This had been offered in an effort to check the drift of population away from the province to the Australian and Californian goldfields. Ring's discovery triggered New Zealand's first gold rush at Coromandel. Forty-two square kilometres around the harbour were leased from Maori owners and the search began. It petered out, however, when it was discovered that the ore could be extracted only by employing expensive machinery.

A second rush in the area in the 1860s proved more lasting and more lucrative. Coromandel and Thames were the centres and both waxed large on prospectors' money. By the 1880s it was all over, however, and the miners and prospectors drifted away or turned their attention to milling or gum digging. Coromandel retains several fine buildings erected during the rush, especially the Gold Warden's Court, which now serves as the County Council chambers. Mine shafts can also been seen around the township, though most are too dangerous to enter.

2. This bay close to Coromandel township is typical of the peninsula's west side. The beaches are more precipitate, tend to mud rather than sand, and look out across the Hauraki Gulf to the South Auckland coast.

3. Wharekaho Beach north of Whitianga lies within the wide sweep of Mercury Bay, the best harbour on the Coromandel Peninsula. The bay was named by James Cook in commemoration of his observation of the transit of Mercury across the sun here in 1769. Cook made careful records of the Maoris and of the settlements in which they lived. It is one of the few areas in the country where archaeology can be linked back to historical records to shed light on how the Maoris lived in pre-European days. The white sand beaches here are typical of those on the east side of the peninsula, which is also more indented than the coast to the west.

Like Coromandel, Mercury Bay prospered initially from the trade in kauri timber and — in its wake — in kauri gum. This gives the area an affinity with Northland. Many individuals and families worked both areas for the same commodities. After the gold rushes the peninsula was found to be rich in other minerals, and this has made it a favourite target for gemstone collectors.

1

2

3

1. Like many seaside communities in the Bay of Plenty Mt Maunganui has a small permanent population that swells by thousands during the summer months as city dwellers head for the coast. It is one of the country's most popular resorts, close to Tauranga city and recognisable from afar by the sugarloaf hill that gives the beach its name.

2. Terns are among New Zealand's most common and most appealing seabirds. Less numerous and decidedly more graceful than the scavenging gulls, they fly in small flocks in search of schools of fish. When they find their prey they fall on them from the sky with unerring accuracy.

3. Hamilton is New Zealand's fourth largest city. It stands on the banks of the Waikato River, the country's largest waterway. Founded by Imperial soldiers in 1864, it was built on the site of a Maori village and group of cultivations known as Kirikiriroa. The Maori inhabitants were driven off as a result of the Waikato War of that year and the subsequent confiscation by the Government of a million acres (405,000 hectares) of their land. The area confiscated turned out to be the richest dairy pastureland in the country. Hamilton grew up largely servicing this new industry. From the mid-twentieth century it became progressively more industrialised and spread its basis of prosperity. It remains more than anything else a river city, and a garden city. The banks of the Waikato have been kept largely in parkland close to the business area and residents and visitors take advantage of this civic asset. Four bridges span the river to link the east bank with the commercial area.

4. In recent years the more torrential North Island rivers — previously not regarded as navigable — have found new popularity as wilderness areas for rafting. Enthusiasts take to the waters to shoot rapids in rubber dinghies. Helmets and lifejackets ensure that accidents are kept to a minimum. This group negotiates the Wairoa River near Tauranga.

4

1. Maori tribes in the centre of the North Island were well known in the nineteenth century for their craftsmanship on water. Lakes and rivers served as a means of transport, a source of food and as a protection against surprise attack. But for the Arawa people, whose headquarters were on Mokoia Island in Lake Rotorua, the lake's waters were insufficient protection against muskets. When Hongi Hika of Ngapuhi swept through here in 1823 he killed 3,000 of them.

2, 3. The best-known river tribes were those of the Waikato. They patrolled their territory by canoe and made war from these craft. During the Waikato War, however, most canoes were broken up by Imperial troops. Seventy years later a leader called Princess Te Puea Herangi revived canoe building as part of her efforts to restore the morale of Waikato Maoris. Although the vessels were never again used for fighting, extensive use is made of them on ceremonial occasions. One of the most popular is the annual Ngaruawahia regatta, held close to Turangawaewae Marae, centre of the Maori King Movement. Here canoes and canoists go through their paces, the participants dressed in traditional costume and using traditional instruments.

1

2

3

4

5

4, 5. In the 1870s the district around Lake Rotorua became New Zealand's first major tourist attraction. What drew visitors from home and abroad was the combination of lakes and springs, living Maori culture and thermal marvels. It was the last of these that evoked most interest. The Rotorua section of the central North Island plateau sits on a cauldron of volcanic activity. In places the ground lid is relatively thin and this activity breaks through in the form of hot springs, geysers or boiling mud pools. The most famous of the geysers used to be Waimangu, which blew itself out in 1917. The best-known now is Pohutu at Whakarewarewa on the outskirts of Rotorua city, which rises over 30 metres. Boiling mud is also a source of fascination for visitors to "Whaka". The process by which it inflates thick bubbles which finally burst and push out concentric circles is reminiscent of simmering porridge. The other attractive feature of the region is the texture of rocks and terraces in the thermal areas, many of them composed of colourful silica. The most famous of these formations were the Pink and White Terraces above Lake Rotomahana, which disappeared in the Tarawera eruption of 1886.

6. Whakarewarewa is also of interest for its close association with Maori culture. Its thermal area is owned by a sub-tribe of the Arawa federation who live there still, sometimes cooking meat and vegetables in boiling pools. Maori guides take visitors around the complex which includes a reconstructed Maori pa with carved posts between the palisades, and an arts and crafts centre.

6

1

1. Tudor Towers, which now houses Rotorua's museum and a restaurant, was once an enormous bath house complex run by the Government. At the turn of the century — in the heyday of spa resorts — the Government was deliberating whether Te Aroha on the Hauraki Plains or Rotorua would be given the nod for official support. Rotorua was eventually chosen, largely because of the additional attractions of Maoris and geysers. This began a long period in which Rotorua was made famous for the allegedly restorative powers of its thermal spring waters. People suffering from arthritis, gout, the effects of strokes and a host of other ailments came to Rotorua to "take the cure". The process was a major foundation of the town's growing tourist industry. Today Rotorua's springs are not lauded as extravagantly, and the Government bath house has closed. Tudor Towers has become a complex catering for more conventional tourist needs and bowls are a popular sport with players on the lawns outside.

2

3

4

2. Rotorua's proximity to half a dozen lakes ensures that visitors get to see a wide selection of waterfowl and other wildlife. Black swans used to thrive in New Zealand but became extinct before the arrival of Europeans, in part because they were hunted by early Maoris. The black swans which now populate the lakes have been introduced from Australia. Native and introduced ducks also congregate in large numbers.

3. Hongi's Track is an exquisite 1.6 kilometre section of road through bush on the Rotorua–Whakatane road. It is named after the Ngapuhi warlord Hongi Hika who cut the track to allow his canoes to be dragged from Lake Rotoehu to Lake Rotoiti. This was in 1823 when he was on his way to attack the Arawa stronghold on Mokoia Island on Lake Rotorua. Previously the area had been known as Te Whakamarura-o-Hinehopu — "the sunshade of Hinehopu". The name had been given in honour of a sixteenth-century Arawa chieftainess who planted a matai tree on the spot where she met her future husband, Pikiao. These two became the progenitors of a major Arawa sub-tribe, Ngati Pikiao. Hinehopu's matai still stands on the track where it is known as "the wishing tree". Travellers are advised by Maori elders to pause under the tree in the course of their journey, to offer a prayer to honour it and to leave a piece of greenery at its base to placate the spirit of the place. Once this is carried out no misfortune will befall the traveller on that trip.

4. South-east of Rotorua stands Kaingaroa, at 150,000 hectares the largest man-made forest in the world. Planting with radiata pine began in 1923, and during the Depression of the 1930s the entire empty Kaingaroa Plains were planted, largely to provide work for the unemployed. The pines mature in about 35 years — two-and-a-half times as fast in New Zealand as in their native California — and are versatile in their use. They now constitute New Zealand's major building material and major timber export.

1

1. The Waimangu ("black water") thermal area is the best-known in the country after Whakarewarewa. It includes the Waimangu Cauldron, a boiling lake that covers more than 10 hectares and is the largest of its kind in the world. The cauldron fills a crater left by a major eruption in 1917 which also blew out the great Waimangu Geyser. Above the lake, wreathed in steam, stand the famous Cathedral Rocks, so named because of their similarity to examples of European gothic architecture. Other attractions in the area include Lake Rotomahana, which was a second crater in the Tarawera eruption of 1886 and which swallowed the Pink and White Terraces, and Ruamoko's Throat, a turquoise lake under scarlet cliffs.

2. The thermal valley at Waiouru was only the second place in the world in which natural steam was successfully harnessed to make electricity. Bores driven deep into the earth capture the steam and pipe it to generators at high temperature and under immense pressure. Water from the adjacent Waikato River is used to condense the steam and intensify pressure, thus creating twice as much electricity as thermal pressure would on its own. The power that results provides about five per cent of the country's requirement. The technology developed by New Zealand in refining this process has

2

since been shared with other countries, particularly in South America. For the visitor to Waiouru the effect of all this is an awesome inferno of noise and smoke that drifts out of the valley and across the main north-south highway.

3, 4. Close to its source at Lake Taupo the mighty Waikato River narrows suddenly to pass through a 15-metre chasm which produces a turbulence of rapids. Below them lie the Huka Falls; above them, nestled into the river bank among protective trees, stands the country's best-known fishing lodge, Huka Lodge, named after the falls. Built by the legendary fishing guide Alan Pye in the 1930s, the lodge used to cater for the rich and the great from all over the globe: Royalty, General Douglas MacArthur, Charles Lindburgh and Barbara Hutton are just a few of those who stayed and fished there. The Queen Mother caught a three-and-a-half kilogram trout there in 1958. Derelict in the 1970s, the lodge was taken over by new proprietors who have given it a reputation for superb gourmet cooking, specialising in game food. Huka Falls themselves are a spectacular spurt of turquoise water. The name, appropriately enough, is from the Maori word for foam. A swing bridge allows visitors to cross the river and view the falls from both banks.

3

4

5. The boat harbour at the north-east corner of Lake Taupo is also the lake's major outlet and the beginning of the Waikato River's 354-kilometre run to the sea south of the Manukau Harbour. Maori tribes who lay claim to the river's bed, however, assert that it actually begins in the Tongariro River, south of Lake Taupo. Speaking in terms of strict geography, experts agree. Prior to the Taupo eruption of about A.D.135 the river flowed continuously from the Tongariro bed to its outlet in the Firth of Thames on the opposite side of the coast to its present course.

5

1

2

3

1. Looking at Acacia Bay on the western shore of Lake Taupo it requires considerable imagination to recall that the lake is the country's largest volcanic crater. When it erupted some 1,800 years ago, it hurled ash all over the centre of the North Island and left a vast hole, into which flowed the Tongariro River. Thus New Zealand's largest lake was created. When Europeans penetrated the district in 1839 the lake was settled and owned by the Ngati Tuwharetoa tribe, led by the famous line of Te Heuheu chiefs. Tribal traditions state that one of their ancestors named Tia discovered the lake and named it Taupo-nui-a-Tia: "Tia's great shoulder cloak."

2. Taupo is best known today as New Zealand's premier fishing resort. Brown trout from Tasmania and rainbow trout from California were introduced in the lake and its feeder rivers in the late nineteenth century. Both varieties adapted spectacularly well to the new conditions. While numbers were low and feed plentiful the fish grew to prodigious size — catches including brown trout over 10 kilograms were not uncommon. Now fish up to four kilograms may be caught more often with the average being about two kilograms. Trolling and casting are both popular and successful on the lake.

3. Taranaki Falls are one of the many varied features of the massive Tongariro National Park and are about one hour's walk from the Chateau Tongariro Hotel. They are formed by a stream dropping 25 metres down an old lava flow.

4. Lake Rotoaira lies behind a natural palisade of cabbage trees below the slopes of Mt Tongariro. It is an idyllic scenic spot reached by two separate routes, one from Tokaanu, the other off the main north-south highway. Unlike Lake Taupo, this waterway and its environs still belong to the Ngati Tuwharetoa people and cannot be fished without a special permit.

The Tongariro Power Project, which gathers water from the headwaters of a number of rivers including the Tongariro and the Wanganui, pumps an additional volume through Rotoaira and on to Taupo. The force created generates electricity in a power station at Tokaanu, and also increases the capacity of older stations on the Waikato River by increasing the flow of water through them. During construction for the project, a nineteenth-century pa site on the shore of Rotoaira was excavated to prevent its being damaged by development. The site is now marked on the Tongariro-Tokaanu road and the results of the investigation can be viewed in the project museum at Turangi. The employment of a professional archaeologist as an integral part of the project was an innovation for New Zealand public works schemes and set a precedent for subsequent ones. As the nation matures its citizens are showing increasing respect for its past and a reluctance to lose relics of its heritage.

5. The Tongariro River is the finest stretch of trout water in New Zealand and its reputation has spread among fishermen throughout the world. This view shows the Red Hut Pool, one of dozens of spots sought by those who know the river. Close by is one of the country's four trout hatcheries. It is used primarily for milking ova from rainbow trout. These are fertilised and then nurtured in incubators for about 18 days, by which time the eyes of the fish are visible. A killing-off process eliminates weaker eggs and those that survive — about five million a year — are sent off to rearing stations in other parts of the country and abroad. In this way the major trout-fishing rivers and lakes are kept stocked with fish.

6. Silvereyes, which enjoy nectar from the kowhai tree, are relatively recent immigrants. They introduced themselves from Australia in the mid-nineteenth century and have spread all over New Zealand and its offshore islands.

4

5

6

1

1. The Tongariro National Park was the country's first, a gift to the people of New Zealand from the Ngati Tuwharetoa paramount chief Te Heuheu Tukino IV in 1887. This was only 15 years after Yellowstone Park in the United States had been established as the first such park in the world. The Tongariro park's nucleus was the three volcanic cones that rise so spectacularly and unexpectedly from the desert of the central North Island plateau: Tongariro (1,968 metres), Ngauruhoe (2,290 metres) and Ruapehu (2,796 metres), the last being the highest peak in the North Island. The mountains were sacred places to Ngati Tuwharetoa, who regarded them as repositories of the mana of the tribe and who also used them for burials. The initial bequest extended to a radius of 1.6 kilometres from all three peaks, an area of 2,600 hectares. Later acquisitions by successive governments swelled the park to its current size of 66,600 hectares. Te Heuheu's initial generosity placed the area outside private ownership and potential commercial exploitation, thus protecting much of its tapu in

2

3

Maori eyes. In addition to mountain skiing, the park offers challenging climbs, long walks through bush and tussock, some 500 species of native plants, springs, small lakes and several waterfalls.

2. Mt Ngauruhoe is the most active volcano on the New Zealand mainland. The Tongariro National Park already offers a paradox of desert and snow, and to this Ngauruhoe adds smoke and steam throughout the winter. The steam and gasses are emitted continuously, and every few years a more spectacular eruption throws out ash and sometimes lava. Since World War II the mountain has had two periods of major eruption. With Mt Egmont, Ngauruhoe is one of the most conical mountains in the world and inevitably invites comparison with Mt Fujiama in Japan.

3. Ruapehu is the only other active onshore volcano in New Zealand. It is a far larger and broader peak than Ngauruhoe and carries the best ski slopes in the North Island on its shoulders. One such ski field is the Whakapapa on the Chateau or northern side of the mountain; the other, Turoa, is on the south or Ohakune side. The Chateau is one of the country's best-known luxury hotels. It stands fortress-like at the base of the mountain. Behind it lie the Whakapapa village, the National Park headquarters, and lower-priced accommodation facilities. Further up the slopes at the Top of the Bruce are a profusion of ski-club huts. Higher still a series of chairlifts and rope tows carries skiers up the Whakapapa field.

1

2

1. The Mokau Falls are but one of several arrestingly beautiful waterfalls that descend into Lake Waikaremoana. The lake (whose name means "sea of sparkling water") lies in the centre of the 211,000-hectare Urewera National Park. Surrounded by the largest area of virgin bush in the North Island, it is also regarded as the most attractive lake in the island. The Huiarau Range provides a backdrop to the north while the spectacular Panekiri Bluff rises a sheer 610 metres from the south. Within the bush can be seen virtually every native North Island plant and land bird.

2. So dense is the bush and so difficult the terrain that the Urewera district remained closed to Europeans longer than any other part of New Zealand. The conservative Tuhoe tribe allowed only a small degree of Pakeha contact at the end of the nineteenth century, and even then it was unwilling. It was not until after World Warr II that the Tuhoe people began extensive contact with the rest of the nation.

3

3. The Mokau River inlet is one of six arms to Lake Waikaremoana, all of which support large numbers of waterfowl. Maoris believed that the lake and its inlets were created by the threshings of a taniwha or river monster trapped in its bed.

4. Far to the east of the Urewera National Park the rising sun touches the East Coast of the North Island, lighting it before any other part of the world on that day. The first peak to catch the rays is Mt Hikurangi, which towers above the Maori township of Ruatoria.

1

2

1. New Zealand's native pigeon is the largest and most colourful of the species anywhere in the world.

2. Taranaki's dairy farmland is equalled only by the Waikato in its capacity for production.

3. The peak of Mt Egmont, still called Taranaki by the Maoris, is often wreathed in mist.

3

4. The Wanganui River flows 290 kilometres from its headwaters in the Tongariro National Park to its outlet in the sea near the city of Wanganui. In the North Island it is second only to the Waikato River in length. Before the arrival of Europeans it was an important artery for Maoris to reach the interior of the country by canoe. Settlements sprang up along its bank and many, such as Pipiriki and Jerusalem, were still well populated in the early years of the twentieth century. Europeans too valued the river's opportunity for transport. A steamer service ran for many years from Taumarunui to Wanganui, the whole journey taking three days. Until it ceased in 1934 this route was regarded as one of the country's grandest scenic excursions. With the deterioration of conditions on the upper reaches of the river such transport disappeared, however, and the remaining Maori communities shrank. By the latter part of the twentieth century they were mere shells, and much of the river was reverting to nature.

5. The site of the city of Wanganui was chosen because there are no harbours on the west coast of the North Island between Porirua in the south and Kawhia in the north. the mouth of the Wanganui River was the nearest thing on that coast to an estuary anchorage and provided a convenient stopover between New Plymouth and Wellington. The area was acquired from Maoris by the New Zealand Company as a result of a dubious transaction in 1840. The town was established the same year and grew to become one of the country's quietest and most beautiful provincial centres.

4

5

1. Mahia Peninsula — a large promontory indented with isolated beaches and dotted with holiday cottages — separates Poverty Bay from Hawke's Bay. Many of these beaches boast the clean white sand so popular further up the East Coast and so different from the black ironsand to the west. Poverty Bay to the north was so named by Captain Cook, who made his first New Zealand landfall there in 1769 at Young Nick's Head. Two days later he set foot on New Zealand soil at Kaiti Beach near the present city of Gisborne. There his crew became the first Europeans known to have witnessed a traditional Maori haka or war dance. And when Maoris ran off with sailors' possessions on two successive days there they became the first of their race to be killed by European firearms. Cook designated the area Poverty Bay because, he said, "it afforded us no one thing we wanted."

2. The Waiomoko River runs into the sea at Whangara north of Gisborne. This area is the gateway

1

2

to the East Coast of the North Island, which some commentators have called New Zealand's Riviera. It is a long stretch of shoreline alternating between rocky headlands and richly sanded bays. As coastal scenery it is perhaps equalled only by the Coromandel Peninsula to the north. Unlike Coromandel, however, the Coast (as it is called) is still pleasingly undeveloped. Because much of the land is still in Maori ownership it has escaped the ravages of subdivision and intensive economic development. In part this is a consequence of the complexities of tribal ownership, which makes development difficult even where people want to proceed with it; and in part it results from a conservative unwillingness of Maoris to interfere too drastically with what has been handed down to them by their ancestors. Where Maori farming has been carried on at the Coast, however, it has been conspicuously successful. This is largely a result of an incorporation system pioneered there by the great Maori leader Sir Apirana Ngata. The results of his blueprint for Maori agricultural and cultural revival can be seen in prosperous small communities such as Tokomaru Bay, Ruatoria and Te Araroa.These communities also have some of the finest carved meeting houses in the country.

3

4

3. In favourable weather and with the right sea conditions, Mahia Peninsula beaches offer superb surfing. So renowned is the area for this activity that in summer surfers head there in large numbers away from other favoured beaches on the west coast. The sport has spawned a sub-culture of its own which embraces clothing, hairstyles, music and magazines, all in addition to the business of surfing itself.

4. Makorori Beach north of Gisborne, and little more than an hour away from the Mahia Peninsula beaches, is another target for surfers in summer.

1

2

1. Cape Kidnappers lies at the southern extremity of Hawke's Bay. It can be reached on foot or on horseback, or by organised safari tours from Napier. In Maori legend it was known as Te Matau-a-Maui, "Maui's fishhook." This referred to the ancestor-god said to have snagged the North Island on a hook made from his grandmother's jawbone and brought it threshing to the surface. The whole island was called "the fish of Maui". The European name was given by Cook in 1769. While his men were trading with Maoris off the cape, some of the locals tried to kidnap Taiata, a Tahitian who acted as servant to his fellow countryman, and Cook's interpreter, Tupaia. Some of the crew fired at the retreating Maori canoe and in the confusion Taiata was able to dive overboard and swim to safety.

2. Cape Kidnappers itself has been likened to the tail of a great tuatara (a lizard-like creature with a serrated back). It is best known for its gannet colony, believed to be the only mainland breeding area for this bird anywhere in the world. The birds formerly nested also on the steeper slope of the point, at some danger to their eggs. But when wildlife officers terraced that section to make it safer the birds abandoned it.

3. The breeding species is the Australian gannet. Like its cousins elsewhere in the world it is a fast and graceful bird, noted for long pointed wings and an exceedingly strong beak. It glides high over the sea in search of food. When it spots surface shoals of fish it falls on them from the sky at speeds of over 145 kilometres per hour.

3

1. Crops such as maize are taking over from more traditional farming in many parts of the country, including here on the East Coast, formerly a prominent sheep-farming area. The East Coast had a special problem. A great deal of the land was in fragmented Maori ownership. This made it difficult to get all the owners together and, once together, to agree on projects for development and production. In addition much of the land was marginal and required large-scale investment to bring it into production. The third problem was that even after these difficulties were overcome and land was carrying sheep or dairy cows, increased mechanisation on larger Pakeha farms often meant that the smaller units became progressively uneconomic. These have been some of the factors persuading owners to seek alternative forms of agriculture, especially crop growing.

2. Rural Hawke's Bay is firmly committed to large-scale sheep farming, the source of the province's early wealth when much of it was in the hands of a small number of station-owning families. The largest stations were broken up as a result of government legislation at the turn of the century. But the district remains oriented to the production of wool and sheep meat.

3. Castlepoint is yet another feature of the New Zealand coast named by Captain Cook, for reasons that are readily apparent.

1

2

Its towering rocks look very like the ruins of a European fortress. It is also one of the few landmarks along the lengthy and relatively featureless Wairarapa coast, which runs from Hawke's Bay to Wellington. In early times Castlepoint was an important meeting place for the Ngati Kahungunu tribe, and an agreement made there with the Te Atiawa from the south ensured the protection of the Pakeha settlement of Wellington in its early days. The point is best known today for its lighthouse. Built in 1913, it stands 22.6 metres high and is 51.8 metres above sea level, making it one of the tallest in the country. Its light is visible for over 30 kilometres out to sea. It is valued especially by ships coming from Panama which have no other identifiable feature to fix on.

4. Castlepoint is also valued by inland Wairarapa residents as one of the few beach resorts accessible to them. Its shelter makes it possible to keep and launch boats there, although the unpredictable action of the sea on this coast has led to fatal accidents. Until the Wellington–Masterton railway opened in 1880 Castlepoint also served as a Wairarapa port. Today one of the most keenly anticipated events for holiday makers is the summer horse races along the beach. In earlier days they were carried on without bridle and saddle. Today riders are more conventionally equipped and wear protective hats.

3

4

CABLE CAR

Wellington

Wellington

Wellington, capital of the nation since 1865, has more sharply contrasting moods than any other New Zealand city. It borders Cook Strait which — in the line of the Roaring Forties — experiences more turbulent wind and sea conditions than other parts of the country's coast. Wellington city often has to bear the brunt of such weather. Wind and tide can eddy round into the harbour with almost uncontrollable ferocity, causing the conditions which sank the vessel *Wahine* in 1968 and which have put a number of other boats on to rocks in the harbour. "Windy Wellington" is the catch-cry — a term of abuse from some visitors unprepared for its gales and held up by the closure of its airport, and of affection from residents who have long since come to terms with the city's vagaries. "At least," they will tell you, "it keeps the streets clean."

In spite of all this Wellington can still turn on —

summer and winter — days of breathtaking stillness and charm. On these occasions a mirror harbour reflects its surrounding hills and the higher ranges behind stand out from the sky with alpine sharpness. On such days and such nights locals and visitors tend to agree that the harbour is the most beautiful in the country, and possibly in the world.

The other immediately noticeable feature of the city is its steepness. But for a small area of flat land — much of it reclaimed — close to the city centre if clings to precipitous hills. And there is no way for the capital to expand but upwards. It is hemmed by a rocky corner of the North Island with water on three sides. Most Wellingtonians seem not to mind. A local poet has noted proudly that it is one of the few places in the world where one could, if one wished, drop apple cores down ships' funnels.

The fact that it is the capital has also had an indelible effect on the city's character. The downtown area is dominated by Parliament Buildings, especially by the new Executive Wing known as the Beehive. Many of the other large buildings are headquarters of government departments. Private companies that have head offices there tend to do so because of the presence of government. The city has always been conscious of the proximity of national political figures. And of course public servants make up a large proportion of the population.

Wellingtonians seem to have fewer opportunities for outdoor recreation than other city dwellers, another consequence of local geography. The parks are few and small and there is no room for new ones. There is, however, an extensive belt of trees ringing the suburban slopes, Oriental Bay with its small beach and Edwardian elegance, good swimming and boating beaches on the eastern side of the harbour, and the golden coast with its resort communities an hour's drive to the north.

1. The first and the most spectacular way to view the capital city is by riding the Kelburn cable car. This unique vehicle lifts travellers from Lambton Quay in downtown Wellington to a superb vantage point above the university and the Botanical Gardens.

2. Oriental Bay is Wellington's only city beach. Although not as large and sandy as places such as Auckland's Mission Bay, Wellingtonians are proud of it and use it in large numbers throughout the summer.

3. Kapiti Island, seen here from the Wellington coast near Waikanae, is the country's best-known bird sanctuary.

3

1

2

1. The Executive Wing of Parliament Buildings is known nationally as the Beehive. It houses ministerial offices and Bellamy's, the MPs' dining room and bars. The basic design was the work of the English architect Sir Basil Spence. It has become one of the major components of the Wellington skyline. Although a source of controversy before and during its construction, Wellingtonians embrace it now even with affection.

2. Another distinctive Wellington landmark is the Carillion, which one professional guide describes as the world's largest salt shaker. It towers from the slope of the city's Mt Cook, close to the National Museum and Art Gallery and above the Basin Reserve cricket grounds. It has a large range of bells which are played from a keyboard, enabling a skilled instrumentalist to coax practically any tune from it in a cascade of bell peals.

3. Red Rocks is typical of the bleak and rugged coastline outside Wellington Harbour. Rock and stone thrown up by movements in the earth's plates have taken a massive pounding from the sea to form sharp fragments, many of the once-horizontal layers squeezed into vertical positions. The seal colony here gathers each year and allows agile visitors to get a close look at creatures that are comparatively rare this far north.

3

4. Fishing in Wellington Harbour is not what it was in earlier years. But enthusiastic youngsters and sometimes ships' crews still try their luck from the Overseas Terminal wharf. The main business area of the city looms behind. In such conditions, with Wellington looking its deceptive best, anglers can expect to catch spotties, mullet and occasionally kahawai. These last are few and far between but well worth the fight they put up when hooked.

5. The Royal Port Nicholson Yacht Club has its boat harbour adjacent to Oriental Bay. Although the city does not support anything like the amount of sailing carried on from Auckland, Wellington yachties are a none the less dedicated group. They claim, in fact, that handling the wind and sea conditions of Wellington Harbour and Cook Strait develops more enterprise and skill than would be acquired sailing in any other part of the world.

6. The harbour's major beach resorts are on the eastern bays, opposite the city. Here yachts put out at Eastbourne, a popular bush-clad suburb and major recreation area in summer. Nearby is Days Bay, where Katherine Mansfield stayed with her family as a girl, and which inspired her story *At the Bay*.

4

5

6

1

2

1. The spectacular sight of Wellington city and harbour in early morning light from the top of Mt Victoria. This favourite spot for visitors and courting couples offers a splendid panorama of the city's unique harbour. The commercial area is spread to the left and centre. The Government centre — including Parliament Buildings, the High Court and most government department head offices — is at mid-right. This view provides a fine vista of glittering lights and reflections at night. The city itself has little nightlife by world standards, and most residents seem to want to keep it that way. When a mayor suggested the capital could benefit from a red-light district he was howled down by an outraged citizenry. This does not necessarily endear the capital to tourists. Most action at night takes place in hotel bars, of which there are a large number, many of them supporting bands. The restaurant scene has improved enormously and cuisine from most parts of the world is now available in both expensive and medium-priced eating houses. The city also promotes an especially lively theatre scene, with two professional companies and several amateur ones offering a continuous and varied range of entertainment.

2. Although Wellington is bereft of parks by comparison with other New Zealand cities, it supports a fine zoo which displays animals and birds from all over the world as well as local fauna.
Here a peacock, proverbially vain, fluffs up his tail feathers in response to admirers' attention.

The South Island

The South Island

In some respects the South Island is so unlike the North that it could be considered a different country. At each extremity it has fiords or sounds made up of high mountains and deep valleys long since inundated by a rising sea. In these aspects the island is more like Scandanavia than a South Pacific region. And there is the great backbone of the Kaikoura Range and the Southern Alps dissecting the land diagonally from north-east to south-west. This feature is not only distinctive in itself; it is responsible for the formation of the glacial valleys to the north and west, the narrow-fingered lakes in the centre of the island and the great alluvial plains to the east.

Even the Maoris have separate origin myths for the south. The North Island was said to have been fished out of the sea by Maui, the mischievous ancestor-god shared by most of Polynesia. The

South Island, however, was believed to be the canoe of Aorangi, son of the Earth Mother and Sky Father. Displeased with their parents' union, Aorangi and his brothers sailed away from Hawaiki, the traditional Polynesian homeland. In the vicinity of the South Island however, their canoe struck a reef and was wrecked. Aorangi and his brothers climbed to the higher side so as not to drown. There, waiting fruitlessly over aeons of time to be rescued by their parents, the siblings turned to stone and became the great peaks of the Alps.

The most common Maori name for the island was Te Wai Pounamu, "greenstone water". It refers to what was in Maori eyes the most precious resource there, a form of nephrite or jade. This stone was prized by Maoris for its fine cutting edge on carving tools and for its highly ornamental quality when worked into items of personal adornment, especially pendants and tiki. The stone was traded from one end of the country to the other.

The top of the island, around Golden Bay, is not unlike landscape further north. It is warm and climatically stable, and many of the limestone formations are reminiscent of those in the King Country in central North Island. The arm of Farewell Spit protects the bay and forms one of the best wading-bird sanctuaries in the country. Tasman Bay too has hot and settled weather, and its beaches have a golden sand that astonishes visitors. "Sunny Nelson" is the provincial centre and it has been able to retain many of its early buildings and much of its charm. The Marlborough Sounds to the east add a range of scenery and maritime opportunities that make the north of the South Island a source of limitless recreational pleasure.

1. Cape Farewell at the top of the South Island was named by Cook as he abandoned New Zealand in 1770 to head for Australia. Close by is the Farewell Spit bird sanctuary, a huge accumulation of sand ground down by West Coast breakers and washed northwards.

2. Kaiteriteri Beach is one of the gems of Tasman Bay. Well sheltered, it has a rich yellow sand unequalled elsewhere in the country.

3. The Kaikoura Mountains hang like a curtain over the rugged Kaikoura coastline on the eastern side of the island.

3

1

2

3

1. Picton is the centre of the Marlborough Sounds. These sunken valleys with their tall hills and deep fiords produce astounding scenery, expecially on still days. The network of waterways was originally charted in part by Cook, who twice based himself at Ship Cove at the entrance to Queen Charlotte Sound, where a memorial to him now stands. Cook also lost 10 men at Arapawa Island in the same sound in 1773. There were no witnesses to this second major clash between Maori and Pakeha. The men went to gather greens and their cannibalised remains were found the following day. Today the area offers endless opportunities for boating and fishing holidays. Its corridors are dotted with cottages, and launches bring mail and supplies to the more isolated outposts.

2. The tuatara is found on several Cook Strait Islands of the north of the South Island. Although lizard-like it is in fact a Rhynchocephalia, a surviving member of the dinosaur family. It grows to about a metre in length and is believed to live for more than 100 years. It is extinct on the mainland and strictly protected on its offshore sanctuaries.

3. The South Island pied oystercatcher flocks on beaches all over the country. Although it migrates and feeds from North

Cape to the Bluff, it breeds only in the south. Despite the name and the long bill it does not feed on oysters.

4. The beauty of Queen Charlotte Sound is especially apparent framed by trees. The bush was luxuriant in Cook's time and his botanist Joseph Banks wrote that the chorus of bellbirds was almost deafening. Today most of the bush has gone — some of it cleared for pastureland, some of it simply cleared and the land abandoned. Increasingly, however, secondary growth is regenerating, and large sections of the sound's hills are being restored to their former glory.

5. Inland from Golden Bay the Heaphy Track meanders through some of the best virgin bush in the country. Named after the pioneering surveyor Charles Heaphy, who traversed part of the district in 1846, the track begins in the rolling Gouland Downs, moves into heavy forest (part of the Northwest Nelson State Forest Park), follows the bed of the Heaphy River to the coast, and finally bursts out of the trees into a magnificent sweep of sandy coastline. It is highly regarded as one of the country's most spectacular walks.

6. The Wairau Valley, inland from the provincial town of Blenheim, has been carved out by the Wairau River. It is the flattest and most fertile district in the north of the island, and is the source of Blenheim's agricultural prosperity. At the mouth of the valley, where the river wanders into a lagoon and then out to the sea, is one of the country's most important prehistoric sites. The Wairau Bar has enabled archaeologists to build up a detailed picture of the life of the earliest Maoris, the Moa Hunters.

4

5

6

1

1. The Golden Bay coastline on the edge of Abel Tasman National Park typifies the qualities that led the Government to set aside the park in perpetuity in 1942. Rocky headlands alternate with sandy coves, and clear water lies off both. The park is a magnet in summer for visitors who want to walk the coastal track or explore the bush behind. Within an area of 22,000 hectares the park offers variety that ranges from mountainous country to lowland bush to offshore islands. It was established to commemorate the 300th anniversary of Tasman's anchorage in Golden Bay.

2. The Buller River, which runs strongly to the West Coast of the South Island, has its headwaters high among the hills of the Nelson Lakes National Park.

3. Nelson's cathedral in the centre of the provincial city has one of the most original towers in the country. The building was unusually long in construction. The foundation stone was laid by Governor-General Sir Charles Fergusson in 1925. But the church itself was not dedicated until his son Sir Bernard Fergusson was Governor-General in 1967. The initial material was Takaka marble, but rising costs and fears generated by the Murchison earthquake in 1929 led to modifications. The planned gothic tower was never built, and the final

2

3

construction material was concrete with a marble veneer. The nearby war memorial — like those in most New Zealand cities — was erected in the wake of World War I, but is used to commemorate New Zealand's participation in all wars.

4. The Maitai Valley is typical of the terrain east of Nelson. Close by is Maungatapu Mountain, scene of one of the country's most notorious slayings. Five men bringing gold dust into Nelson were killed there by the Kelly gang in 1866.

5. Shags — known as cormorants in other parts of the world — are prolific on the New Zealand coast and rivers. This one is at Collingwood in Golden Bay.

6. Lake Rotoiti is the focal point of the Nelson Lakes National Park. The other lake there is Rotoroa. Both are surrounded by steep hills which make up the bulk of the 57,000 hectare park. Rotoiti is more popular with boat users and offers more amenities.

5

4

6

Canterbury

Canterbury

The Canterbury Plains make up the largest single area of flat land in New Zealand. Formed by the deposits of widely sweeping rivers — especially the Waimakariri, the Rakaia and the Rangitata — they provide a fertile base for agriculture. The region is the major one in the country for grain growing. It is also the home of Canterbury lamb, long regarded as the best meat New Zealand produces and exports. Originally sheep were established there for wool-growing only, but the advent of refrigerated shipments to the United Kingdom in 1882 opened up a major overseas market for New Zealand meat and turned growers interests in that direction.

The higher country to the west (the foothills of the Southern Alps) is covered largely with tussock. Early efforts by run holders to burn off native vegetation for replacement with grass created

2

massive problems of erosion which have proved difficult to repair. In this area, especially in the Mackenzie Basin, lakes excavated by glaciers are a major tourist attraction and an important source of hydro-electric energy, particularly at Ohau, Tekapo and Pukaki.

Further west along the chain of the Southern Alps stand the country's great peaks. Seventeen of them exceed 3,000 metres, with the highest, Mt Cook, reaching 3,764 metres. They provide opportunities for scenic flights, for climbing, for skiing, and they are an ever-present backdrop to the lakes and townships at their feet.

The centre of Canterbury, however, is Christchurch. Founded in 1850 as an Anglican settlement by the Canterbury Association, Christchurch is more English-looking than other New Zealand cities: it has its square based on the Cathedral, the River Avon meanders through it with flower- and tree-lined banks, it has spacious parks, and it is well known for the beauty of its private gardens. In fairness it should be said that Christchurch also has industrial and manufacturing areas which produce carpets, machinery, textiles, leather goods, fertilisers, clothing and footwear. It is not all pretty and nostalgic in its aspects and prospects.

To the east of the city, over the Port Hills, lies Banks Peninsula, scenically stunning and sparsely populated. A system of ancient volcanoes, the peninsula is characterised by high hills, deep valleys and narrow inlets around the coast. The port of Lyttelton is the major settlement; others include Akaroa, Governors Bay, Diamond Harbour, Port Levy and the Maori pa of Rapaki.

Major towns to the south are Ashburton, Timaru and Waimate. Inland from these the most visible network of roads in the country intersects the plain, crosses its rivers and provides the means by which grain, meat, wool and vegetables can be carried out to markets in other parts of the country and abroad. Oddly for an area so swept by water, low rainfall and porous soil require much of the interior farmland to be extensively irrigated.

1. Christchurch, the flattest city in New Zealand, lies spread on the Canterbury Plains. The plains were laid down by soils swept off the Southern Alps and spread by a series of fanning rivers.

2. The River Avon, seen here flowing through the Christchurch Botanical Gardens, is responsible for much of the city's English appearance.

3. Christchurch's port of Lyttelton Harbour is set in an ancient volcanic crater on Banks Peninsula. It is linked to the city by the Lyttelton tunnel under the Port Hills.

3

1. Sumner Beach lies on the southern arm of the estuary formed by the Avon and Heathcote Rivers. It was originally planned as a resort for the citizens of Christchurch, which does not have a beach frontage. Sumner today is mainly of interest for its volcanic rocks and caves, especially the famous Cave Rock formed by the action of sea on ancient lava. In Maori legend the rock is identified as a petrified whale or as a taniwha. It is topped by a flagstaff that was used in earlier days to signal the state of the estuary to incoming ships. At nearby Redcliffes, Sir Julius von Haast in 1872 excavated the floor of one of the country's earliest cave shelters which led to important discoveries about the nature of Maori settlement.

2. Christchurch is blessed with one of the largest and most beautiful city parks in New Zealand. Hagley Park provides residents with a haven of peace only minutes from the city's centre. It has tree-lined walks, tow paths, tracks for joggers and horses, playing fields, a golf course, the Botanical Gardens and the Millwood Reserve, an area of shrubs and flower beds known especially for its rhododendrons and azaleas.

3. Akaroa Harbour is one of several deep indentations in Banks Peninsula that provide excellent anchorages and shelter for settlements. It also adds a unique Gallic flavour to New Zealand's story. The village was founded in 1840 as the country's only French settlement. The colonists arrived to find that British sovereignty had just been declared. They remained there, however, although the French company who owned the settlement sold out to the New Zealand Company in 1849. The French influence remains visible in Akaroa street names and in the names of Canterbury residents descended from those original colonists. Akaroa is also known for the extent to which it has retained its early architecture by preserving its late-Victorian cottages.

1

2

3

4

4. Small craft ride peacefully on safe Akaroa moorings. The harbour formerly contained a major settlement of the South Island's Ngai Tahu tribe, who used its waters to shelter and beach their canoes. Those same waters gave access to enemies, however. Te Rauparaha of Ngati Toa descended from the North Island in the trading ship *Elizabeth* in 1830 and captured the leading Ngai Tahu chief, Te Maiharanui. Ngati Toa canoes also reached Onawe Pa in the harbour two years later and the crews destroyed the settlement and ate many of the inhabitants.

5. The Christchurch Estuary provides a sheltered stretch of water on which most of the city's regattas and yacht races are held.

5

1

1. Lake Pearson, resting below the snow-clad Craigieburn Range, provides a glimpse of classic South Island landscape. Right along the east side of the Alps glacial action carved out the lakes, blocked them with silt and then filled them with water as the glaciers retreated. Lake Pearson, shaped in a flattened figure eight, is one of the smallest. It is named after Joseph Pearson, the first European to explore the area in the 1840s.

2. The Waiau River is one of the South Island's best trout- and salmon-fishing waters. It is pictured here close to Hanmer Springs, named after one of the district's early Pakeha settlers. When first located by Europeans in 1859, the thermal springs were set in bare tussock country. Early bathers hoisted an item of clothing up a flagpole to indicate which sex was in occupation of the pools. Later the area was developed as a spa, and judicious planting of exotic trees gave it a resort-like appearance. Queen Mary Hospital carried on hydrotherapy here until

2

3

1971, when the institution was turned over to the treatment of alcoholics.

4

3. Lake Tekapo is one of the South Island's scenic climaxes. It is known especially for the colour of its water, described as milky turquoise. This is caused by the suspension of rock dust ground by glaciers and carried into the lake by its feeder rivers. The surrounding countryside is largely tussock land, dotted with only occasional trees. To the west lie the foothills of the Alps. The gentle slopes around the lake make excellent ski fields and the area is now as popular with winter tourists as it is with summer ones. The lake lies in what is now known as the Mackenzie Country, called after a Scottish sheep stealer who allegedly took his illicit flocks there in the 1850s. His pursuers found the wide, golden tussock valleys that now bear the Scottish name, and it was opened up for English and subsequently Scottish settlers, most of whom raised sheep. The Mackenzie Country is beautiful in a desert-like way, the wind-scorched tussock reflecting a golden glow.

4. Further south in the Mackenzie Basin Mt Cook looms high over Lake Pukaki.

5. In winter Lake Tekapo presents a snow-bound aspect that some people have found European in its composition.

5

1

2

1. The first skiing in New Zealand was attempted in 1893 inside what is now the Mt Cook National Park. Today skiing is still carried on there but it is — from necessity — alpine skiing. The best run is that down the Tasman Glacier. Planes carry tourists and skiers to the head of the glacier, where the latter then have a fabulous 13-kilometre trip in front of them down to Ball Hut. The glacier, some 29 kilometres long and nine kilometres across at its widest point, is the longest in the country and the largest in the world to be located in a temperate zone. It is followed by the Murchison (17 kilometres), the Mueller (13 kilometres) and the Godley (also 13 kilometres). Altogether there are some 360 glaciers in the Alps, a higher number than in the European Alps.

2. Several of the South Island's major tourist hotels were deliberately sited near glaciers. Best known is the Hermitage, built near the Mueller Glacier in 1884. The original structure was destroyed by flood in 1913 and its successor by fire in 1957. The present building is one of the

3

finest hotels in the country and attracts thousands of visitors every year. The introduction of alpine flights from the hotel over the Mt Cook National Park has given a new dimension to the area's appeal.

3. This mountain buttercup is one of dozens of rare alpine plants to be seen within the borders of the Mt Cook National Park. So varied is the vegetation that many botanists come to the park in spring and summer simply to walk the slopes in search of flora.

4. Mt Cook, at 3,764 metres, is the highest peak in New Zealand. Although its Maori name Aorangi has often been translated as "cloud piercer", South Island Maoris more commonly attribute it to the name of the ancestor-god reputed to have discovered the region by canoe. The mountain was called after the great navigator James Cook but not by Cook himself. The name was bestowed by Captain J. L. Stokes who completed the first survey of the New Zealand coast in the early 1850s. The first serious attempt to scale the mountain was made in 1882 by Swiss climbers who got to within 60 metres of the summit. The first successful attempt was made on Christmas Day 1894 by three New Zealand climbers, spurred on by the news that an English mountaineer with a Swiss guide was coming to the country specifically to attempt the climb. Even with the passage of years and the growth of mountaineering experience in New Zealand it remains one of the country's most challenging climbs.

4

1

2

3

1. An enthusiast on the Tasman Glacier skis down to Ball Hut after being dropped higher up the slope by plane. In general South Island skiing is better than that available in the north, and attracts more visitors from Australia and elsewhere overseas. In addition to the Tasman other favourite locations are Coronet Peak, Mt Hutt, Craigieburn Valley, Tekapo, Mt Cheeseman, Porter Heights, Erewhon and Awakino. Of these Coronet Peak has the most advanced facilities.

2. Lake Ohau on the border of Canterbury and Otago is another popular South Island ski resort. The surrounding hills fall gently towards the lake and provide ideal slopes for beginners. The Lake Ohau Lodge hotel serves as a base for the sport in winter, while in summer it acts as a fishing lodge (the lake is also well stocked with trout). Above the lake and to the north stands the Ben Ohau Range, revealing a poetic blend of Maori and Scottish traditions. In Maori legend the lake itself was formed by the weeping of two brothers whose sister had drowned at the mouth of the Waitaki River. Their tears created the lake, which in turn led to the formation of the Waitaki as its waters flowed out towards the sea.

3. Mt Sefton is another peak that is popular with climbers inside the Mt Cook National Park. It was first conquered in 1895, the year after Mt Cook was scaled. Since the 1890s the area has been used extensively by New Zealand and Australian climbers, frequently at a high cost in loss of life. It has also served as a training ground for climbers who went on to make their mark elsewhere in the world: most notably for Sir Edmund Hillary, the New Zealander who in 1953 became one of the first two men to climb Mt Everest in the Himalayas, and for New Zealanders who have taken part in Antarctic expeditions.

The West Coast

The West Coast

The West Coast of the South Island is almost a country within a country. Although much of it — especially the old province of Westland — is on the same latitude as Canterbury, and although it shares a view of the same alps, it could not contrast more sharply than it does with the South Island's eastern seaboard.

There is the terrain, for example. Where the Canterbury Plains are flat and cultivated, the West Coast is hilly and rugged. Where the plains are wide, the lowlands in the west are narrow and always close to the sea. Where the east has ports, the west has none except river mouths, of which only Greymouth is navigable — and even it is often closed by inclement weather. Where the east coast is remote from bush and mountains, the west has both in close proximity, with the slopes of the Alps falling sharply westwards to the sea. It is this close

relationship of forest and mountains, and forest and glaciers, that gives the West Coast some of its most spectacular scenery, and acts as a magnet for visitors. The best-known glaciers — Fox and Franz Josef — are in retreat, but they still extend close both to the coastal road and to the hotels built to capitalise on their beauty.

Much of the Coast is cloaked in dense forest, especially kahikatea and beech. Strong lobbying by conservationists has resulted in a great deal of it being preserved in perpetuity as part of the country's National Parks system. One area, Okarito Lagoon, is the sole breeding place for New Zealand's rare white heron and the even rarer royal spoonbill. Little lakes such as Brunner, Kaniere, Ianthe and Mapourika make up a chain of scenic gems.

Although the population on the Coast is low now, it was a boom area in the middle of the nineteenth century. The discovery of gold there in 1864 brought miners in their thousands from older fields in Otago, Coromandel and Victoria. It also attracted large numbers of Irish immigrants, another point of contrast with the more anglicised province to the east. As the gold ran out other industries were established around coal and timber and these preserved a measure of prosperity for a time. But as these extractive activities exhausted the most accessible resources by the early twentieth century, the level of prosperity and the population declined sharply.

The West Coast today presents a face of dereliction and of nature reasserting itself. The communities that remain are small but strong, independent, loyal to the Coast and hospitable in a manner that has become proverbial for its generosity. Increasingly, the area is sought out by visitors from other parts of the country and from abroad who want to experience an alternative New Zealand to that which they find elsewhere in the country.

1. Characteristic West Coast scenery shows an alpine backdrop, bush-clad foothills, a swampy river flat and tall native pines. Here Mts Tasman and Cook can be seen from close to the Fox Glacier.

2. The stretch of shore near Punakaiki is typical of terrain on the West Coast between Westport and Greymouth — a bleak and windswept area pounded by the sea and only sparsely populated.

3. The famous Pancake Rocks at Punakaiki are made of stratified limestone worn by the action of sea and wind into weird shapes.

3

1 

1. After Arthur's Pass the road from Canterbury falls steeply down through the Otira Gorge, gateway to the West Coast. The gorge is the most important link between the island's east and west settlements. It includes the portal of the tunnel which carries the railway connection under the mountains. The gorge has long been a favourite with photographers and landscape artists attracted by the spectacular scenery afforded by deep folds in the foothills of the Alps and a large variety of sub-alpine vegetation.

2. Harihari, 19 kilometres south of Hokitika, is a typical West Coast farming community. It lies in a flat

2

3

4

river valley surrounded by steep bush-covered slopes, and it supports a timber mill. It was close to this spot that the first solo aerial crossing of the Tasman ended in 1931. Guy Lambton Menzies of Sydney flew his single-engined Avro Avian for 11 hours and 45 minutes to finish his journey upside down but safe in a swamp near Harihari. Once he was recognised the settlement gave him a hero's welcome.

3. Greymouth on the Grey River provides one of the few safe anchorages in Westland. The town became the major port for the Coast in the nineteenth century and was especially important for the shipping out of coal. The river bar, however, remains unpredictable and dangerous.

4. Weka or woodhens, rare in or absent from other areas of the country, thrive in parts of the Coast. These confident and inquisitive birds often go to great lengths to explore and search for food. They will enter huts and tents and stick their heads into cupboards and rucksacks. Their victims regard them with exasperated affection.

5. Lake Brunner is one of the most attractive of Westland's chain of little lakes. Surrounded by bush it provides a pleasant venue for swimming, boating and trout fishing.

5

1. The bush track around the perimeter of Lake Matheson is one of the easiest and most enjoyable walks on the West Coast. The lake was formed by a large slab of ice left behind by the retreating Fox Glacier some 14,000 years ago. The ice was insulated from the ground by a layer of gravel, and hence took a long time to melt. As it did so it slowly collapsed the gravel and sunk a massive depression into the earth. When it filled with water the depression became the lake.

2. Kaniere is another of Westland's small lakes. It too is popular in summer with swimmers, boat owners and picnickers. Water skiing and trout fishing are additional attractions. At the nearby town of Kaniere visitors can view huge tailings left behind by one of the last gold dredges to work on the Coast. More than 4,900 kilograms of the ore were extracted from the area.

3. Typical West Coast rain forest shows lush tree growth and a profusion of mosses and lichens. It takes an exceptionally high annual rainfall to sustain growth of this kind.

1

2

1

2

1. Mt Tasman and Mt Cook seen from the western side of the Alps. To the left the Fox Glacier drops towards the coast. The Alps fall away far more sharply here, giving rise to some unexpected and beautiful juxtapositions of mountains, bush and coastline.

2. Lake Matheson on an early spring morning provides its famous reflections of Mt Tasman and Mt Cook. With its fringe of bush, this West Coast scene is now a classic one.

3. The Fox Glacier cascades down the slopes of the Alps to end only a few kilometres from the coastal highway. Although like other South Island glaciers it is in retreat, there is still more than enough of it to surprise and delight visitors to the Coast.

3

Dunedin

Dunedin

More than any other city in New Zealand Dunedin has preserved its Victorian features by retaining many of its early houses and civic buildings. This gives it a distinctive character and a decided charm, and is a source of loyalty from residents and delight for visitors. Of the buildings perhaps the university is the most spectacular. It was the first to be set up in the country, in 1869. The slate roofs and bluestone walls are reminiscent of long-established British universities and date from 1879.

The city was founded at the head of Port Chalmers, which was itself an important settlement for South Island Maoris. By the late eighteenth century the Ngati Mamoe and Ngai Tahu tribes were fighting regularly in the area as the latter sought to establish pre-eminence. Violence became inter-racial as sealers called at the harbour and in many

instances treated the Maori inhabitants abominably. In return the Maoris took revenge, and not necessarily on the Europeans who had initially attacked them. Even today the Otago Peninsula (rendered Otakou in Maori) is a major headquarters for the Ngai Tahu people and one of their best-known pa stands near the head of the point.

The European chapter of Dunedin's history began in earnest with the formation of the Otago Association in Scotland in the 1840s and the establishment of "New Edinburgh" on the site of present-day Dunedin in 1846. The bulk of the first settlers were Scottish, many of them members of the Free Church. Their leaders were Captain William Cargill (after whom Cargill Hill overlooking the city from the north is named) and the Rev. Thomas Burns, a nephew of poet Robert Burns. Although English and Irish immigrants eventually put the Presbyterians in a minority, the Scottish character of the city largely persisted. Most of the influential city fathers were for the remainder of the nineteenth century those of Scottish origin, and they controlled the city's banking and engineering activities. Even today the Scottish antecedents are apparent in street names, in the southern dialect "r" sound, and in such city monuments as those to William Cargill and Robert Burns.

The Otago gold rush in the 1860s brought the city a burst of prosperity. Money from the fields at Gabriel's Gully, Dunstan, the Shotover and the Arrow River all passed through Dunedin, adding to its wealth and enabling the construction of many of its finest buildings and houses. Commercial activity has declined in the city in the twentieth century, however, as investment money has moved north. Dunedin today is a viable but not an expanding community. Much of its appeal for visitors comes from its architecture, its cultural institutions such as the museum and the Hocken Library, and its scenic points around the harbour, especially the albatross colony at Taiaroa Head.

1. Otago Harbour seen from the heights of the Otago Peninsula. The peninsula's length and the size of its hills provide the best anchorage in the southern part of the South Island, and were the major factor in the choice of a site for Dunedin in the 1840s.

2. Woodhaugh Gardens is one of Dunedin's parks that preserves a peaceful and rural atmosphere close to the city's streets.

3. Larnach's Castle was begun in 1871, the work of local Member of Parliament William Larnach, who became Colonial Treasurer, Minister of Public Works and Minister of Mines.

3

1

1. Moeraki on the coast north of Dunedin was the site of an important shore whaling station in the 1830s. It also became a Maori settlement as Ngai Tahu people routed by the Ngati Toa raids from the north abandoned their old homes and formed a new community. Many of them intermarried with Europeans at the station, thus forming some of the best-known South Island Maori families. On the beach close to Moeraki Point lie many of the famous Moeraki Boulders — huge spherical rocks as much as four metres in circumference and weighing several tonnes. There have been many explanations for the phenomenon. One researcher from overseas has claimed they are evidence of a visit to earth by extra-terrestial beings. Maoris identified them as petrified food baskets from one of the ancestral canoes that brought them to New Zealand from Hawaiki, the Polynesian homeland. In fact they were formed on the seabed some 60 million years ago by the accumulation of lime salts around a small centre. They fall from an eroding bank behind the beach as the softer coastal mudstone weathers away.

2. Dunedin's Scottish heritage is most dramatically apparent in the statue of Robert Burns that dominates the city's Octagon. One of the co-founders of the community was a nephew of the poet, and annual Burns' Suppers are held there still. Behind the statue stands St Paul's Anglican Cathedral, another landmark, built from Oamaru stone at the turn of the century.

2

The South

The South

The south of the South Island has several features that have been developed more fully than in the country as a whole. One is tourism. Based on the extraordinary juxtaposition of lakes and alpine scenery, the south attracts an increasing number of visitors each year. Queenstown on Lake Wakatipu is the major centre, but the other lakes — Te Anau, Manapouri and Wanaka — all draw their share. Ski resorts, expecially Coronet Peak, add to the appeal. And in summer trout fishing, boating and swimming in the lakes are further assets. Fiordland to the west would also be an additional drawcard if its sounds were more accessible. As it is, most visitors there head for Milford Sound, which has one of the best hotels in the country. They travel by road, by air or on foot via the fabulous Milford Track. Breathtakingly beautiful Dusky and Doubtful Sounds are more difficult to reach.

The lakes and rivers of the south have made the region a vital one for the generation of hydro-electricity. This water power comes from many of the southern lakes, and from the massive Clutha and Waitaki Rivers. Round the coast fishing and crayfishing constitute a major industry, while the Bluff oysters of Foveaux Strait are world-famous for their delicacy of texture and taste.

Inland, the valleys of Central Otago have developed as a major fruit-growing region and are known especially for their peaches and apricots. Agricultural development in Southland was difficult at first because of large areas of swamp which needed draining before land could be brought into production. But intelligent development programmes were devised and the area now carries an increasing number of sheep and cattle with each successive year.

The region suffered from its first boom – caused by the Otago gold rushes — in the sense that it was too narrowly based to provide broad development. Once the gold had gone it was a long time before alternative sources of income took its place. Slowly, however, the south has established an equilibrium through a combination of agriculture, fishing, tourism and some manufacturing industries in Dunedin and Invercargill. The aluminium smelter at Bluff, which uses cheap local power to process Australian bauxite, has also made a major contribution.

To the far south, across Foveaux Strait, Stewart Island remains the last large undeveloped part of the country — a chance to see the New Zealand landscape as it was when it was wholly given over to birds and bush. And there is a national determination to preserve it this way.

1. The incomparable Milford Sound (presided over by its aptly named Mitre Peak). According to South Island Maori legend the gods placed viciously biting sandflies here to prevent humans becoming hypnotised by the beauty of the view. The sound can now be reached by road, by air and by foot, the last option over the well-known Milford Track.

2. Wanaka is another in the succession of South Island lakes with a mountainous backdrop. It feeds the Clutha River which, in its lower reaches, contains a greater volume of water than any other river in the country.

3. The Clutha Valley flats near Tarras, built up over centuries by deposits from the Clutha River.

3

1

2

3

1. Lake Wanaka from Glendhu Bay. The landscape around Wanaka is more smoothly planed by glacier action than that around other lakes. The effect is one of softness, certainly gentler to the eye than some of the more spectacularly rugged South Island views. In legend the lake was carved out of the earth by Te Rakaihautu, who travelled all over the South Island with a digging stick looking for wells. Other examples of his handiwork were said to be Te Anau, Manapouri, Wakatipu, Tekapo and Pukaki. The name Wanaka is an example of poor transcription by Europeans. The lake was named after an early Maori chief in the area, Oanaka. There is a township named after the lake close by.

2. The Cardrona Valley seen here from the Crown Range highway was formed by the Cardona River flowing out of Lake Wanaka. It was the scene of a major gold rush in 1862, which left ugly scars on the landscape at the time. Now much of the valley is manicured with grass, flowers and English trees.

3. Lake Hayes, close to Queenstown, is the best trout-fishing water in the district. It too has been framed and tamed by exotic trees in preference to native ones.

4

4. Waterfall Park near Arrowtown is named for its best-known feature.

5. Arrowtown is the best-preserved relic of gold-rush days to be found in New Zealand. Its miners' cottages and town buildings have been kept relatively intact from the 1860s. The Lakes District Centennial Museum — formerly the Arrowtown Bank of New Zealand — is the focal point with its pictures, furniture, mining tools and other paraphernalia from the town's boom days. The Arrowtown Gaol — much needed on account of the general brutality and lawlessness of goldfield behaviour — is also preserved. The rush that gave birth to Arrowtown began when gold was discovered on the banks of the Arrow River. The discovery was kept secret for some considerable time, but rumours of its existence began to spread when gold in large quantities was taken into Clyde by furtive prospectors, especially by an American named William Fox. As other people discovered him at work on the Arrow, Fox swore them to secrecy and dealt them in on the arrangement. The existence of the field was finally exposed when a group too large to be terrorised or controlled came upon Fox and his men in 1862. From that time the rush was on and Arrowtown sprang up virtually overnight.

5

1. The Treble Cone ski ground above Lake Wanaka offers the highly prized South Island powder snow. The North Island ski fields, which slush and ice over frequently, have nothing to compare with such conditions. Treble Cone also gives an unparalleled view of the lake and its surrounding country, which is touched with snow for a large part of the winter months.

2. With some 29,000 hectares of surface, Lake Wakatipu is the second largest lake in the South Island (after Te Anau) and the third in the country. Its major settlement is the tourist resort of Queenstown, which is viewed most spectacularly from the Bob's Peak cableway. In the background stand the Remarkables, a range of mountains that produce a stunning effect when they are dusted with snow. Queenstown was originally established as a sheep station. It mushroomed into a township during the Wakatipu gold rush of the 1860s. After the gold had been exhausted residents began a

1

programme of planting and beautification to give the district an alternative attraction and source of income, and this has paid off handsomely. Some have called it the most beautiful town in New Zealand.

3. For years many of New Zealand's most rugged and boulder-strewn rivers were inaccessible to boat travellers. This was changed by the invention in the South Island of the Hamilton jet boat, a vessel of shallow draft able to propel itself speedily and safely into some of the remoter parts of the country. Jet-boat journeys have become a major feature of the South Island tourist industry. Here visitors ascend the Shotover Gorge not far from Queenstown. This river, the major scene of the Wakatipu gold rush, was named after a property of the same name near Oxford.

4. Coronet Peak above Queenstown is the country's best-known and most heavily patronised ski field. From the peak itself (1,619 metres) to the lower slopes its dry powder snow is prized. Further drawcards are the beauty of nearby Queenstown and the comforts and accommodation it offers. The skiing season here extends from July to September. Buses bring sports enthusiasts to the lower slopes from Queenstown and a chairlift carries them up a

2

3

4

further 450 metres, almost to the summit. For movement about the lower slopes there are poma lifts and ski tows. The chairlift also operates during the summer so that visitors can take advantage of the views at that time of the year too.

5. The steamer ***Earnslaw*** which carries tourists across Lake Wakatipu is all that remains of a fleet of boats that used to ply the lake in the nineteenth century. They transported passengers from Kingston at the south end to Queenstown and Glenorchy to the north. Their patronage was guaranteed because there was no road around the lake until the 1930s, and the railway went only as far as Kingston. The last-but-one survivor of the fleet was the paddlesteamer ***Mountaineer***, which operated for nearly 60 years before being withdrawn from service in 1932.

5

1

2

1. Some of the most rewarding but also the best-hidden scenery around Wakatipu can be found at the head of the lake, on the Glenorchy road. Here, approaching Glenorchy, Mt Earnslaw rears up, unusually isolated in comparison with other South Island peaks. The steamer on the lake is named after it.

2. Lighthouse Rock is one of the dominating features close to the precipitous Skippers Road. The Skippers Gorge was the scene of one of the country's most arduous gold rushes. Conditions in the steep narrow valley were at times appalling. It was reached by a dangerous bridle track, from which horses and men frequently fell. Once in the gorge miners had to struggle constantly for footholds as they panned and prospected up bleak ravines. Winter conditions were especially punishing as icy winds swept through the gorge and deposited snow. Many men perished here and were left behind in the Skippers Cemetery. For all this, many prospectors still believed the result was worth the effort and the danger. Gold was found in quantity and quality. The miners claimed that each square foot of the bed of the gorge yielded up at least an ounce of ore. Such a reputation meant that in addition to the privations supplied by nature, over-crowding was another. Chinese workers also came here in large numbers, especially to re-work parts of the bed that European prospectors had passed over quickly and not always thoroughly. The road through Skippers today is scarcely less frightening than the original bridle track. It is narrow and tortuous and hangs over enormous drops in places. It should be attempted only with patience and care.

3. The Eglinton Valley runs close to Lake Te Anau on the road to Milford Sound. Its thick bush and alpine prospects provide one of the most rewarding drives in the country.

4. This sight of the Sutherland Falls is one of the highlights for walkers

3

4

of the Milford Track. Dropping 580.3 metres in three stages, the falls are the highest in New Zealand and among the highest in the world. They are named after their discoverer Donald Sutherland, also known as the Hermit of Milford, who was the first person to live permanently at the sound.

5. Another popular resting place on the Milford Track is the Giant Gate Falls. Many of those who have completed the track declare that it is the finest walk in the world.

5

1

1. Lupins bloom on the shore of Lake Manapouri. The lake became the subject of controversy in the 1960s when the Government of the day prepared to raise it for the generation of electricity. A national outcry prevented this measure and it remains today largely unspoiled.

2. Queen's Gardens in Invercargill is the Southland capital's major park.

3. First Church in Invercargill points to the city's Scottish antecedents. It was named after the founder of Dunedin, William Cargill.

4. Dawn at Halfmoon Bay, Stewart Island, the only inhabited part of New Zealand's most southern coastline. When Cook first circumnavigated the country in 1770 he made in this region one of his few major mistakes in charting: he believed that Stewart Island was attached to the South

2

3

4

Island and rendered it so on his map. It is not known for certain when the error was discovered and rectified, nor exactly how the island received its name. Certainly by the turn of the nineteenth century sealers were calling at the island and, later, whalers too landed there. Most early exploitation of the island was for its timber, which was milled until the turn of the twentieth century. Tin and gold were also mined for a time at Port Pegasus.

5. The settlement of Oban in Halfmoon Bay is the only one on the island, its permanent population a little over 300 people. Most of them draw their living from the sea, from commercial fishing. In summer the numbers swell with an influx of South Island visitors, many of whom own cribs (holiday cottages) in the bay. The island is linked to the mainland by the ferry ***Wairua*** which crosses from Bluff several times a week. There is also an air service from Invercargill. There are no roads, apart from one around Halfmoon Bay, so travel around the island is necessarily by launch or on foot.

5